*100 years of the C A West & Son*

*Memoirs of a Farmer*

Published by
John Nickalls Publications
Oak Farm Bungalow, Sawyers Lane, Suton, Wymondham, Norfolk,
NR18 9SH.


First impression : December 2010

ISBN 978-1-904136-32-3

Design and typesetting :
Tim Smith www.spacepenguin.co.uk

Front and back cover:
Old and New: Tractor driver Chris Jude is now a pensioner but
still drives the big tractor and plough. He is also seen on the back
cover driving the beet harvester some 50 years ago.

# FOREWORD

I am probably one of the oldest inhabitants to have lived in the local villages all my life. My mother's family, the Flowerdews, followed William the Conqueror from Normandy and have farmed in this area, until recently, ever since. The Wests arrived here from Surrey in 1908 and are still here. They were two farming families that originally had very different backgrounds.

Listening to my forebears, I am able to record the vast changes in the market towns and countryside in recent times. By recording these changes in this book, readers, especially those who have moved here recently, will become aware of the great differences and contrasts that have taken place over the last century.

Above: Church Farm House, Brome, a photograph taken by Cleer Alger circa 1850s. My wife Sylvia and I have lived here since 1952.

Below: E.D.P. photograph taken when I was county chairman of Norfolk Farmer's Union, 1985

# CONTENTS

Great Grandfather Flowerdew, 1840, Ivy House Brome. Copy of a portrait painting.

# "Oldest Couple" Married 75 years Ago To-day HE IS 99, SHE IS 95

Evening Standard Correspondent, 1940

Said to be England's oldest married couple, Mr. James West, who will be 100 in October, and his wife, 95 in December, of Milland near Midhurst, Sussex, celebrated the 75th anniversary of their wedding to-day.

Of their 14 children, 10 are still alive; they don't know how many grand-children or great grand-children there are.

During 60 years on the little farm Mr. West has produced his own meat, milk and vegetables, while "Mother" has baked bread and made butter and cheese.

"Jimmie," as Mr. West is called, started work as a bird scarer and has never had a doctor's bill.

Both he and his wife are in good health, and attribute their longevity to "plain living and good, wholesome food".

Mr. and Mrs. West (Great Grandfather West)

George Flowerdew in mayoral robes, Eye

Charles Augustus West

Oliver and Hannah West with Peter and Michael

# INTRODUCTION

I was appointed village historian of Brome and Oakley some 30 years ago, and in that role I have come across records revealing the lives of the Iceni, Romans, Saxons, and Normans who lived here, along with people who have lived here during my time.

Now approaching my 82nd year, and having lived and farmed in the North Suffolk/South Norfolk area all my life, I feel the many changes in rural and farming life should be recorded.

While this is not a definitive history of farming in the early 20th Century it is the history of two farming families, the Flowerdews and the Wests.

My Great-grandfather James West, born in 1840, was the son of a farm labourer working in Sussex. Conditions were very harsh at this time for farm workers, and when his father was out of work he had to take his wife and family of four to the Easebourne workhouse. The 1851 Census described them as paupers.

When James left school he went to work as a farm labourer on the 80-acre Waldergrove Farm, in Chithurst, Sussex. He married the farmer's granddaughter and they eventually inherited the farm. They were to have 14 children. My grandfather, Charles Augustus West, was their eldest.

For my other Great Grandfather on my mother's side, Arthur Flowerdew, it was a different story. He was born in 1836 at Ivy House Farm, in Brome, into a privileged family. His father was farming 500 acres. The 1841 Census of Brome shows that his mother and father had three children living there as well as a governess, three female servants and one male servant.

By coincidence my grandfather Charles Augustus West lived there from 1928 until he died in 1958.

On Arthur Flowerdew's marriage to Hannah Symonds he moved to Billingford Hall, on the Norfolk/Suffolk border. His mother, before she married was Emily Blomefield, her family had already been living there for 100 years. They were descendants of Francis Blomefield, the 18th Century Norfolk Historian.

By another coincidence Arthur and Hannah were also to have 14 children, 10 boys and four girls, the eldest of which was my grandfather George Flowerdew. But unlike the children of James West the boys were all educated at Framlingham College.

These two farming families were the forebears of what was to become C A West and Son.

A meeting of the hunt at Oakley Park in the early 1900s. The timbered park covered 200 acres in Hoxne and Oakley

One of the 10 gamekeepers showing his vermin pole, proving he was successful in controlling the predators in his area. Records show that about 5,000 pheasants were shot in a month

Brome Hall in the early 1900s, showing the extensive gardens and the mansion

The Eye entrance to Brome Hall, a mile-long avenue of oaks followed before the hall was reached

# CHAPTER ONE

## *The farming families on the Brome and Oakley Estate*

One hundred years ago my father Oliver West, aged four, arrived with his mother, father and sister at Warren Hill Farm, Oakley.

At the same time my mother, Hannah Arete Flowerdew, was born at Gissing Farm, Hoxne, where her father was farming. Both farms were on the Brome and Oakley Estate where my grandparents were tenants.

At the time the estate was a huge operation. To get some idea of just how big it was we can take a look at the estate records, which were found virtually untouched for 30 years, when in 1955 my Grandfather bought Eye Abbey and its farm.

The records covered the period of the Kerrisons' era going back to the 19th Century. We cleared the estate office and I retained some of the records, while the rest went to Ipswich Museum. One hundred years earlier the estate owned more than 7,000 acres spread over 12 villages, and consisted of 288 houses, 38 farms and many small holdings and allotments were tenanted.

In Brome and Oakley 88 houses were on the estate. The only farm, which was not in their ownership, was the Parke's Farm in Brome – their family had been owner/occupiers for 200 years.

Living in Brome Hall was Agnes Burrell, known as Baroness Bateman, who lived there after the death of her brother Sir Edward Kerrison, who was the second baronet. His main residence was Oakley Park, and he only resided at Brome Hall occasionally.

Hiring the park at this time was the Hill-Wood family (they also owned Arsenal Football ground). The rent was £1,000 per annum. They employed three gardeners and 10 gamekeepers as well as the domestic staff.

Incidentally the park house was just to the east of Oakley, in Hoxne, and the park was in the two parishes. On the Brome Hall estate tenant farmers were paying on average just over £1 per acre rent per year. This included their house and farm cottages. Other tenanted cottages were averaging about £4 per annum rent, most were paying a further 10/- for allotments. The average wage for estate workers was around £2 a week. This included carpenters, bricklayers, wood men and general workers. Winter hours were 6.30am to 5pm with one hour for meal breaks.

During the summer an extra half an hour was worked. On Mondays work did not start until 7am and on Saturdays work finished at 4pm.

Income for the estate came from rents for houses and farms.

Farming went into decline around the time of Sir Edward Kerrison's death in 1886. The estate was managed by the trustees for Lady Bateman, and accounts seemed to indicate that outgoings were exceeding income. After her death the estate was put on the market to be auctioned. Much remained unsold and after a second unsuccessful auction in 1921, the estate went into liquidation.

Farming ceased to be profitable, unemployment was rife and agricultural workers' wages were reduced to 26 shillings per week.

At the present day nearly all the farms and houses are owner occupied.

Brome Hall and Oakley Park are now attractive modern houses. If grants for the renovation of these two historic mansions had been available at the time of their sale, they would most probably still be in the original grounds in their original form.

Fernhurst Water Mill at the time of Charles West's first business in 1887

Warren Hills, Oakley, in 1911 with Charles and Elizabeth West with children
Oliver (my father) and his sister Ruth

# CHAPTER TWO

## Grandfather West's start in Farming and Milling

My grandfather Charles Augustus West arrived on the Brome and Oakley Estate 100 years ago. The eldest of 14 children, he was born in 1868 on his father's 80-acre farm in Chithurst, Sussex.

Charles had to leave school at the age of 10 as his father wanted him to work on the farm. He received no wages and at the age of 17, being dissatisfied with his status he was persuaded by relatives to emigrate with them to Florida, in the United States. Other relatives gave him money for his fare and a gold sovereign to spend when he arrived.

As he was preparing to leave for The States he became aware of a smallholding and a watermill at Fernhurst, just a few miles from his home which was vacant and in need of a tenant.

His father hired the property and with his fare money to America he was able to start up in business using the mill to process animal feed, which he sold along with other commodities. He never spent the gold sovereign and it is now in the possession of my grandson George West.

Now he was in business. The mill was used to process animal feed, which he sold with other agricultural commodities. He also started a contracting service buying a corn binder, which was new to the area. This was not a popular move as it put 10 hand reapers out of work. Such was the strength of feeling that he had to pay someone to protect it at night to prevent it being vandalised.

In 1901 at the age of 31 he married my grandmother Elizabeth Hansford. She was the daughter of the landlord of the local pub, called the Spreadeagle, in Fernhurst. By now he was hiring a farm at Haselmere, in Surrey, while his brother Len was running the mill at Fernhurst.

Charles and Elizabeth moved to Haselmere, and this was the birthplace of my father Oliver.

At this time Grandfather was selling Fison's fertiliser from the mill. The manufacturing factory was in Ipswich and the agent informed him that farms in Suffolk were being rented out for less money than the land in Surrey.

He decided to investigate and in 1908 he hired Warren Hill Farm on the Brome and Oakley Estate.

The annual rent was £477-9-0. This was for 530 acres, a farmhouse and six farm cottages. He hired a goods train, and he and Len brought all the livestock, farm implements and mill parts from Sussex and Surrey to Diss by rail.

This move from Sussex and Surrey to Suffolk earned my grandfather the nickname of Surrey West, but he was not the only farmer to move into the area at this time. A number of Scottish families – the Lauries, Alstons, and Blacks – moved here and as livestock farmers they brought with them new ways of farming. Their descendants are still here, just like Surrey West's.

When my grandfather moved into the Brome and Oakley estate my other grandfather George Flowerdew was already farming on the estate, having hired Gissing Farm, in Hoxne in 1902.

The prosperity of farming towards the end of the 19th Century was in decline and food was being imported from the New World at low prices.

Billingford Hall tea party in 1914. My aunt Roa sits next to her sister Arete, great grandmother and grandparents (seated). Seated are my uncles Dick, left and Ken.

Four generations of the Flowerdews in 1930. George and Hannah Flowerdew with their daughter Arete and me as a one-year-old

In 1890 Grandfather George decided to emigrate to Canada and worked his way across the continent, and headed south into America, finishing up in California, searching – unsuccessfully - for gold. He then moved to Australia and joined the police force there, considering it to be a more secure occupation than gold prospecting.

A few years later he moved to New Zealand, there he met my grandmother Hannah Moore who was farming there with her two brothers. They married in New Zealand in 1901 and shortly afterwards returned to England.

On his return he found that his brother Frank was running the estate with his father, both were still living extravagantly.

Grandfather decided to set up on his own and hired Gissing Farm, in Hoxne and after a few years hired Oak Lawn Farm, in Eye, as well as keeping some of the Hoxne land.

Great Grandfather Flowerdew died in 1915 and Frank, in 1920, had to give up the farms.

Frank and many other farmers in the area were losing money in the 1920s.

The traditional methods of farming in East Anglia had become unprofitable resulting in many agricultural bankruptcies and the collapse of the big farming estates.

The survivors were the ones who were prepared to change and adapt to the changing market.

Pig and dairy farming became profitable using cheap imported feed stuffs and sheep farming became more prevalent as the animals were used to graze the abandoned arable fields, which were then converted to grass.

Gordon Flowerdew, on the right, who emigrated from Billingford to Canada, pictured in Oakley Park with his cavalry brigade in 1915

Death and Glory: Alfred Munnings dramatic impression of the charge of the Strathconans at Moreuil Wood led by Gordon Flowerdew who is remembered on the war memorial in Billingford Church. Seventy percent of the cavalry men were killed or wounded, but they succeeded in forcing the German Army to retreat. Flowerdew was awarded the V.C. posthumously.

Len West, in the foreground, is baling straw ready for despatch to the horses in France. Charles Augustus is in the trilby, centre, Oliver West is behind the bale.

R33 moored on its mast on our farm in Dickleburgh. The giant hangars appear close, but they are in fact half a mile away in Pulham.

# CHAPTER THREE

## *The Great War and beyond*

The Great War brought huge changes to the locality and no more so than on the estate in Brome and Oakley.

During the war the estate housed much of the Canadian Regiment called The Lord Stathcona horse. Some 1,200 cavalry horses came from Canada with the regiment. I found records at the Eye Abbey Farm Office of a rifle range and camps in Brome, Oakley and Hoxne.

Grandfather West who was a farm contractor at the time won a contract to service these horses with hay, straw and feed.

When the horses were transported to France in 1917 he baled the hay and straw, which was then sent to France via the local railway stations and shipped over the Channel.

Stationed at Oakley Park was Gordon Flowerdew – brother of Grandfather Flowerdew – who had emigrated to Canada some years earlier. My mother often spoke of her Uncle Gordon exercising the horses on the roads and fields in the area. All these horses and cavalry must have had just as much impact on the local communities as the airfields did during the Second World War.

Gordon lost his life in 1918 fighting in France.

Meanwhile great changes were taking place at Pulham, Dickleburgh and Rushall: The Admiralty had bought 900 acres of farm land in these parishes. One square mile of land was cleared, all ditches were filled in and the land flattened to create an airship base. Some 68 fields became one expanse of grassland with no obstacles to impede the airships' landing.

This was twice the area of the airbase, which was constructed in Brome and Eye during the Second World War.

Workshops, hangars and living quarters were built. The personnel on the site at one time exceeded 3,000. The base was to be used for airships, which the locals nicknamed the Pulham Pigs because of their shape.

These airships were used to search the North Sea for submarines and the German navy.

It was on this airfield that Grandfather West hired, in 1915, the grassland to make hay for the army horses and graze his sheep and cattle.

Towards the end of the war the smaller of the airships were being replaced by much larger airships, over 600ft long and 80ft high. Two large hangars were built covering five acres of ground each. They were huge – they were 120ft high as they had to house the monster ships. They were to dominate the landscape for years to come.

A mooring mast 120ft high was also erected to land these monsters.

The first airship – the R34 – to cross the Atlantic in 1919, landed on this mast at Pulham. It was piloted by Major Scott, who was later Commander at Pulham. He flew from Edinburgh to America, and then returned again to the base at Pulham.

This was only one week after Allcock and Brown had become the first people to cross the Atlantic by air. They landed in a bog in Ireland.

My father, who was working with sheep there, often recalled the day in 1924 when the R33, sister ship to the R34, broke away from the mast in a gale.

He was working nearby with the sheep when the ship sailed over him with mooring gun carriages dangling below, just skimming him and the sheep.

It took more than 24 hours to bring the ship down to earth again.

After the war life was no less hazardous for the livestock and workers alike.

The airships were used to drop dummy bombs on targets; parachutists were jumping from the airships and landing near the grazing animals, they even practised flying biplanes after they were released from being suspended from the airships.

All these experiments were not very successful and Pulham was downgraded in the late 1920s.

One hangar was dismantled and reassembled at Cardington, Bedfordshire. The remaining hangar was bombed in 1940 and was dismantled in 1947.

With such activity out of the way grazing livestock and farm work became more peaceful.

During the first Great War Grandfather hired three more farms from the estate in Brome and Oakley as well as the Pulham airfield. His brother Leonard and later his nephew Stan participated in the contract work, which by this time was considerable.

Tractors and lorries were replacing horsepower and he established a machinery and storage depot on sites, which are now homes to Morrisons supermarket and the John Grose Ford garage on Victoria Road, Diss. He also went into partnership with the Cooper family, who owned a garage on a site which is now Somerfield in Mere Street, Diss.

When the 1914-1918 war ended a large number of ex-servicemen were returning to civilian life and for many of them finding employment was very difficult.

Grandfather's philosophy was to employ any one who could earn him a shilling. Deep down I think he was very conscious of the fact that while returning men had experienced suffering and hardship in the trenches, he had been successful in his contracting work and wanted to even things out.

One of the returning servicemen was a man called Wallace King, a former sergeant in the army. Grandfather decided to finance him to enable him to purchase redundant Army and Airforce stores and equipment.

The five-acre site south of Park Road, Diss, was soon filled. Wallace bought aircraft hangars from the Thetford area and re-erected them on the Diss sites. A store in Crown Street was also purchased to sell ironmongery and surplus stores. Wallace later expanded into the furniture and general stores covering East Anglia.

At Grandfather's death the sale of Wallace King shares helped to pay the death duties. About this time Mr Cooper retired and Grandfather's nephew Stan West was put in charge. The garage was an agent for Rolls Royce and Austin cars and also Austin and Case tractors. Eddie West, another of Grandfather's brothers became a salesman for Rolls Royce.

Listening to his tales he was very successful visiting large country houses in East Anglia and selling his wares in a rather unorthodox manner. His customers were regarding motor vehicles as horseless carriages and he persuaded them the Rolls Royce was the only thoroughbred.

He was well aware of the wealth in this area, so when the boom in car sales waned, he went into the hotel trade.

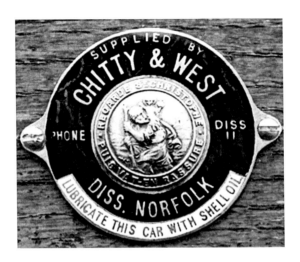

The first Chitty and West tractor demonstration, Autumn 1927

# CHAPTER FOUR

## *The long post-war recession*

The downturn in fortunes also affected agriculture in the 1920s with the price of farm produce falling quite substantially. This brought much hardship to the rural community. Looking at the farm records it appears that the price of grain, livestock and wages had all fallen to below pre-war levels. Farming once again was in depression. Oakley Park and its farms were auctioned in May 1920 and Brome Hall and farms a year later.

After Lady Bateman's death in 1918, attempts to sell the estate as a whole had not been successful. It appears that tenants in the 12 parishes of Eye, Occold, Braiseworth, Thrandeston, Yaxley, Brome, Oakley, Stuston, Hoxne, Denham, Billingford and Horham had all been given notice to quit in Michaelmas 1920. About half the farmers on the estate bought their farms before the day of the sale and I have no records as to the fate of the tenants of the 280 houses on the estate. My grandfather was offered the chance to buy his 950 acres of tenanted land at the same time as receiving his notice to quit. He made an offer which was refused and he prepared to move to the Park House, on Mere Street, in Diss.

He believed his five acres of properties in the centre of Diss were worth more than his tenanted land in Brome and Oakley, the assumption of his made in 1920 is probably still the case today.

Neither auction was successful. The mansion in Oakley Park was bought for demolition. (Brome Hall was not sold, and the estate went into liquidation in 1922). Grandfather Flowerdew bought Gardner's Farm, in Eye (next to Oak Lawn Farm) at the second sale. He paid £25.00 per acre for the farm including the farmhouse and buildings. It had been withdrawn at £40.00 an acre at the first sale. The Liquidator organised a sale of the contents of Brome Hall in December 1922, the sale lasted five days.

Brome Hall and the remaining 450 acres were finally auctioned in September 1924. Sir Thomas Tacon, a well-known resident of Eye, was the purchaser.

Mere Street, Diss in 1927 showing the petrol pump kiosk and Park House

Telephone No. 11
Telegrams : " West's Garages, Diss "

11752

MERE STREET AND PARK ROAD GARAGES

DISS, *July 31st 192 7*

M *.....................*

DR. TO **WEST'S GARAGES**

(C. A. WEST)

MOTOR AGENTS AND ELECTRICAL · ENGINEERS

Invoice showing petrol at a shilling a gallon (20p). Grandfather was selling his mil
for the same price. Petrol is now five pounds and milk is being sold by farmers for
one pound a gallon. We no longer sell milk.

The Garages,

## Mere Street, and Park Road,

# DISS.

Catalogue of

# 75 Private and Commercial Motor Vehicles

comprising

## 50 MOTOR CARS

including late model Austin, Clyno, Essex, Ford, Morris, Riley, Standard, Sunbeam, Wolseley, Vauxhall, and other Saloons, Coupes, 2-seaters and Touring Cars, in first-class running order, also many older models in good sound order and without reserve.

## 20 COMMERCIAL VEHICLES

including the following on LATEST MODEL FORD CHASSIS, 'Flexion' Six-wheeler Chassis.

14-16 seater Saloon Bus. Furniture Van. 30-cwt. Truck.

New Body for Ford 30-cwt. Truck.

### 4 Six-ton A.E.C. Long Wheel base LORRIES

on pneumatic tyres.

DAIMLER 3-ton CHASSIS on pneumatic tyres.

### CADILLAC BREAK - DOWN LORRY.

Ford (model T) Vans, 1-ton Lorry, Crossley Light Lorry,

**TWO FORDSON TRACTORS**

(one of which is new, used for demonstration only.)

**Wallis and E.B. Tractors and Implements.**

### MOTOR CYCLES

Car Engines, Parts, Tyres, Oil and Accessories.

Petter 100-volt & Lalley 30-volt Electric LIGHTING PLANTS

Motor Lawn Mower, Electric Washing Machines, Wireless Sets, Cash Register, Duplicator, Typewriter, Toy Rover Motor Car, 3 EXCELLENT LATHES. Garage Pumps and Equipment. Steel and Wood Oil Barrels, and Miscellaneous Effects, which

## THOS. WM. GAZE & SON

Are favoured with instructions from Messrs. Chitty & West, to Sell by Auction, upon the Premises,

## On TUESDAY, MAY 19th, 1931.

Commencing at 11.30 punctually.

NOTE— The Vehicles comprised in this catalogue may be sold before the date of sale and others purchased—no liability shall attach to the Vendors or the Auctioneers if any advertised vehicle is not present for sale.

CATALOGUES may be obtained of the Auctioneers, Crown Street, Diss, Norfolk, or of Mr. W. D. Chitty, at The Garage, Diss.

Garage surplus sale in 1931

The old Brome village hall before it was demolished in 1975. It was built in 1926 using two railway carriages

Grandfather West, in the meantime, had bought his tenanted land from the official receiver. Grandfather added to his farm purchases at the auction and bought, for £610, six houses and 25 acres of land, making the houses worth £70.00 each and the land £10.00 per acre. The six tenants of the houses were paying annually £24-4-0 or one shilling and seven pence per week each. Looking at the price of land over the next 10 years £10-00 per acre seems to be the average price paid in this area.

The purchased farms were soon to see the ex-army buildings, which were not used in Diss, being erected to house Grandfather West's dairy and pig enterprises. In those days one did not need planning permission for such a change of use.

At this time innovations were coming into the dairy industry with the introduction in the 1920s of milking machines.

In Diss, Geoffrey Brame started an electrical business in the garage on Park Road, Diss. He later had his own very successful radio and television business on Market Hill.

Railway carriages were also being dismantled or converted for storage and living accommodation.

In Brome two railway carriages were converted to build a village hall and villager Wilf Plant lived happily in another carriage in Brome Avenue for many years.

Ex-Army and old ex-London buses were stripped down and converted to lorries for road transport. These lorries were used to collect farm produce directly from the farms to deliver to the London markets of Smithfield and Covent Garden daily.

Milk was also collected this way and transported to the milk depots. Grandfather had established a market for his milk in London, whilst farming in Surrey.

During the summer there was a surplus of milk and he purchased a dairy business in Great Yarmouth and transported milk daily from Diss during the holiday season.

Animal foodstuffs imported from abroad were transported back from the docks to the farms and feeds mills in the area. In 1926 the railways, as a result of a labour strike, came to a standstill for six weeks. Grandfather West at this time was employing 28 lorry drivers. Road transport was the only means of getting food supplies to the towns. From then on the goods transported by rail diminished and many road haulage firms flourished.

At this time Leonard West had taken a farm at Lopham, Stan West had returned to Sussex having bought a garage there and Eddie West was in Bedfordshire in the hotel trade.

Bill Chitty had appeared on the scene and taken over the management of the Diss Enterprise. I think he rationalised a hotchpotch of businesses. Austin and Case Tractor agencies were replaced by Fordsons tractors and Ford cars replaced the Rolls Royces. In 1927 the firm became known as Chitty and West.

In the late 1920s and early 1930s Grandfather had heart problems and my father Oliver took on the responsibility of running the farms, which at the time were losing money. Grandfather, I believe, quite unfairly blamed my father for the losses, as most farms in the area were in the same position. Grandfather had been ill, but as his health improved in the early 1930s, he decided to relinquish his influence in the Diss business and it became known as W.D. Chitty.

His remedy for the losses in farming was to expand and I have a note in the farming press that in 1938 he was farming 5,000 acres.

With this in mind I decided to analyse the accounts of C.A.West & Son of Ivy House, Brome in June 1938.

My father, as well as getting a share of the profits was receiving the same wage as the head herdsmen and foremen – two pounds, 10 shillings per week, there was a total of 108 employees. At that time the farm inventory included 65 horses, 415 dairy cows, 888 other cattle, 1809 ewes in three sheep flocks and 650 pigs.

During the year 442 cattle, 1692 sheep and 1839 pigs were sold. I believe all these animals sold were destined, eventually, for the meat trade. Milk created the biggest income, followed by pigs, then cattle and sheep.

Only 584 acres of the farm were devoted to arable cash crops: 68 acres of Brussel sprouts was the biggest earner, followed by 134 acres of sugar beet.

The 307 acres of barley and 75 acres of wheat was way down the list. Wheat was sold at £9-00 per ton and barley £12-00. The straw was most probably worth as much for use by the livestock as the grain itself.

A further 236 acres of arable land was devoted to feed for the livestock. Some 93 acres of Lucerne, red clover and rye grass, for cattle and horses, 40 acres of beans for young stock, 20 acres of oats for horse feed, 30 acres of tares (sheep feed) and 53 acres of kale and marigolds for the cows.

The sugar beet crowns and leaves were also fed to the cattle and sheep, and in the spring the sheep pens for lambing were set up. For lambing adjacent to the sprout fields, this fed the sheep until the grass grew again in the spring.

The rest was very rough pasture, some being abandoned arable fields, and others very wet marshland. Drains and dykes were no longer being maintained. I remember going with Father round the Brome Hall farm in 1936.

Harry Peck had been the farmer on Brome Hall Farm in 1934 and he became bankrupt. After that the farm remained idle. Grandfather paid £10 rent for the first year and £40 the following year. The farm was 250 acres and had many farm buildings.

Harry continued to live in the farmhouse, and work on the farm. He and his wife had been leading figures in the village. People were very sympathetic and this role was to continue.

I can remember other instances where C.A. West & Son either bought or hired farms and allowed the farmer to continue working the farm. At this time, I frequently went with Father and Grandfather to inspect the livestock, by now the farm covered a wide area of Norfolk and Suffolk.

There was land in East Harling, Snetterton, Shelfanger, Pulham, Dickleburgh, Rushall, Palgrave, Eye, Orfordness and Halvergate Island, as well as the original Stuston, Brome, Oakley and Hoxne land

Scole Blacksmith shop on the main Norwich to Ipswich Road. It shows Ted Hardy, who served in Italy, and Charley Parr, killed in the blackout in Scole while serving as a special constable. 1938 EDP picture.

Diss Railway Station in 1938, showing horses which were used for shunting goods and livestock wagons in the station yard.

Building and thatching corn stacks during harvest

Threshing at Oakley in 1938

Mere Street, Diss

CHAPTER FIVE

*Life on the farm in the 1930s*

I was brought up on Warren Hill Farm, which was the centre of activity. There were 14 farm cottages on the farm in Oakley and 15 in Brome – all originally part of the Brome and Oakley Estate. Ten council houses had also been built on the farm and most of these housed farm workers. At the time none of the houses had running water or electricity. The toilets were all at the bottom of the garden. The Oakley workers came to Warren Hills, some on bicycles, some walked.

The stables, housing 16 very large Suffolk Punches, were very near to our back door. I would often be in the stables when they returned from work and would help with the feeding.

There were no health and safety officers then to reprimand me. I learned at a very early age that I could only be near the older more docile horses and keep well clear of the younger horses being trained.

By the age of 10 it was my responsibility to take the older horses to the blacksmith's in Scole in the school holidays and on Saturdays, this added five pence to my pocket money of seven pence. Scole Blacksmith's shop is no more having been replaced with three bungalows next to Scole Church. The Blacksmith's shop was then beside the main Norwich to Ipswich road, and horses being on the road waiting to have their shoes fitted was a common sight and caused traffic hold-ups.

At this time a narrow humped-back bridge crossing the River Waveney divided Oakley from Scole. Steam lorries going from Norwich to Ipswich would often stop here to take water on board before continuing their journey. Another memory of the bridge was riding with my father in a steam engine pulling a threshing drum and straw pitcher from Pulham to Warren Hill, the engine stalled on the bridge blocking the road.

Father had run out of coal and we had to walk to the farm, get more coal and get steam up to continue the journey. This caused the road to be closed all afternoon.

The narrow arch of this bridge caused three major floods in the Diss, Scole area: 1938, 1947 and again in 1967. On each occasion houses were flooded. My father was a county councillor at the time and he campaigned to get a new bridge built and the old one demolished. When this was accomplished the risk of flooding in this area was greatly reduced.

I have noticed that our land in Stuston does not flood so frequently, with the water flooding lower down the river and spilling onto land at Billingford, Thorpe Abbotts, Hoxne and Oakley more often. Houses here are not at such a high risk of flooding.

In 1938 Warren Hills was a hive of activity and my father Oliver was now in charge of most of the daily activities on the farm. I should explain that back in the 19th Century two quite large farms were on the site being farmed by the Pike family: one was in the village of Brome, the other in Oakley. To confuse matters further both had the postal address of Scole. Warren Hills, at that time, was considered a hamlet.

Father was living in the Oakley farmhouse. Beside the stables was a very large barn. Behind these buildings Grandfather had built two very large First World War sheds. One housed farm implements and tractors while the other was for pigs.

On the Brome farm the barn was used as a mill and mixing plant for the use of the livestock. The ingredients were usually by-products from the flour mills from London and Ipswich as well as cheap imports from the docks, sometimes there would be five lorries a day in the yard.

At this time road haulage business was booming, taking farm goods to the towns with return journeys coming back to supply the mills. There were four large mills expanding in this area: Savills at Mellis; Smiths, at Dickleburgh; Tucks at Burston and Burroughs at Bressingham.

Grandfather had erected three more of his large buildings behind the mill. One housed the dairy herd of about 90 cows. These were all individually tethered for feeding and milking and needed a labour force of six people. The milking machine was installed in the 1920s and all the milk had to be carried to the dairy, where it was cooled.

There were five other farms with a milking herd, on one the cows were still being milked by hand.

The other two sheds at Warren Hills were used for pig fattening, making three in all. A number of large scale pig fattening units were springing up at this time, I believe the pioneer of this system was David Black at Bacton.

There was a small breeding unit at Poplar Farm, in Oakley, but most of the pigs in the system came with purchase of store (half grown) pigs from the many small holdings in the area. On occasion I went with Grandfather on his purchasing visits to these small holdings. We were always made welcome.

He would visit four or five farms in a morning, making sure he could get a lorry load of pigs. These small farms were very diversified with the wife usually feeding chickens and pigs while the farmer had a few cows which were hand milked.

There would be two horses capable of pulling a one-farrow plough, a corn binder and a small Smythe drill, built locally at Peasenhall. This drill was very versatile, capable of drilling grain, mangels and sugar beet, as well as small seeds. Each of the three fattening sheds at Warren Hills would have three lots of pigs pass through them in 12 months. Each batch of arrivals had to be segregated. Swine fever was rampant at this time and the police had powers to visit farms to see the segregation regulations were carried out.

Feeding the pigs was the most unpopular work on the farm. Their food, ready mixed at the mill, would be placed in large tanks beside the piggeries and soaked with water, then bucketed into round pig troughs in the yards.

The pigs showed no respect for their feeders, jostling the buckets. In 1945 I kept pigs on Brome Airfield in Second World War army sheds and developed a much easier method of feeding with bulk dry feeders.

## CHAPTER SIX

### *My early memories of school and farming*

I first went to school at the age of five in 1934. It was a large private establishment called Entry House, opposite Diss Primary School. Father took me to school by car and I returned on the bus, which was a daily service between Diss and Eye via Scole and Hoxne. The bus was always parked near the Mere.

My days on the bus ended when, for my eighth birthday I received a bike. After that I always biked to school daily.

The pre-war journey to school was much different to that of today. I probably did the journey on my bike more quickly than I do now in a car. A traffic jam in Diss was unheard of – unless the Wests were driving their livestock through the town.

Stuston Common was used for grazing. David Laurie had a dairy herd, which returned to the farm at nights. Other Common graziers penned their cattle at night on a paddock next to the Golf Club. A full-time keeper was employed by the commoners to prevent the animals from straying.

Over the bridge Ernie Orford had a pub- now the White Elephant. Behind the pub was his slaughter house. The farm used to deliver animals there in a horse-drawn cart, which would hold two bullocks or 10 sheep or pigs. On the corner was John Wyatt's haulage business. He was also a pioneer for Caterpillar tractors doing contract work on farms.

The railway station road was always busy with coal and goods being delivered to surrounding villages and farm produce and other goods being delivered to the station. Goods trains were as frequent as passenger services and horse transport out-numbered motor transport. On the left side there was a large Maltings, and further along Young's Ironworks, which was engaged in the manufacture and repair of farm machinery. Opposite there was the Gas Works with two very large cylinders on the skyline.

Diss street lighting was powered by gas and a man on a bicycle carrying a long pole was employed as the gas lighter – having to light and extinguish each one every night. Further along Victoria Road was a horse drinking trough, which was as busy as a petrol station is nowadays.

On Fridays, Diss was a hive of activity as it was market day and Diss had the busiest town centre in the area. Apthorpe's had a livestock market stretching from Park Road to Denmark Street; Gaze's had markets on both sides of Roydon Road. There were two poultry markets as well, one on Shelfanger Road and another on Mount Street.

In the afternoon Diss Corn Hall would be packed with merchants and farmers trading. Every merchant hired a large upright desk with a stand which kept him a little higher than his customers. These desks were stacked around the edge of the hall when there were other functions. At the back of the hall or upstairs there was usually an auction of a farm or houses and property in these rooms on a Friday.

An early picture of Gaze's lamb sale. The horse drawn auctioneers wagon was the wagon my grandfather rode on in the 1930s

I have vivid memories of Gaze's Annual Lamb Sale during which more than 10,000 lambs would be sold and the pens covered the whole of the sale ground meadow. Practically all the lambs arrived on foot.

I always went with our consignment, taking a day off from school. Victoria Road was a sight with flocks of lambs being driven every 200 yards and the sheep dogs keeping the different farm animals apart.

Diss lamb sale claimed to be the largest one day sale in England, bringing in the progeny of flocks covering a wide area around Diss.

Some of the lambs were destined to be fattened on other farms in the area, but the majority were driven to Diss Railway Station, their destination being to farms further afield to be either fattened for slaughter or to be used for breeding. The sale pens would cover the whole of the sale meadow, on Roydon Road.

Grandfather being the largest consignor, would sit on the auctioneer's horse and wagon and watch the auctioneers, Clement Gaze and his son John sitting at their desk selling whilst the wagon would move up and down the many rows of lambs, which were penned in temporary pens erected using locally made hurdles with sharpened ends knocked into the ground. One year Clemet Gaze lifted me onto the wagon and introduced me to the crowd as a future flock master. This was never to be as our last sheep were sold in 1941.

My early memories of Pulham Airfield are ones of a vast area of featureless grassland. The milking cows were confined to an area around Vaunces Farm, where my nephew, Duncan West, now farms. The First World War buildings had been converted for the use of livestock. Living in the farmhouse was Mrs Scott, the widow of Major Scott, an Army officer in the First World War. He was in command of the airbase until he was killed in the crash of the R101 Airship in 1931.

In the middle of the grassland was a huge airship hangar covering more than five acres and 120 feet high. Other First World War buildings and living quarters were still present. The second airship hangar had been dismantled and rebuilt in Cardington, in Bedfordshire.

About this time the narrow gauge railway line, beside the mainline junction, was being extended to service 48 storage sheds being built at intervals on the grassland. 200 acres were fenced in, and, for a time, our cattle and sheep were excluded.

The sheds were constructed for the use of the RAF to store munitions and this area became known as the Danger Area. We were offered alternative grazing land for our cattle on Orford Ness - a spit of land stretching 10 miles from Aldeburgh to Shingle Street. This was also RAF land.

I have memories of 200 cattle being driven from Oakley to these marshes, a distance of about 25 miles. Roadside hedges were still in place and there was little motor traffic on the roads at that time. On the first day, four drovers and two cattle dogs would walk the cattle along the narrow roads and would rest them overnight on grazing land in the Snape area. On the following day most of the cattle would be driven through Aldeburgh and up the beach to the marshes. On the third day the remaining cattle were driven to Orford past the castle to the banks of the River Alde, opposite Halvergate Island. The cattle were then loaded on to a barge 15 at a time and taken across the river. The cattle did the return journey in the Autumn by the same method.

The barge had been in use for a number of years. A very thick rope was secured on the island and then threaded below the landing door on the barge to the mainland landing post. The cattle were loaded and then the barge went to the island, powered by two men hauling on the rope. I always went with my father on these three days in his car. It was the highlight of my Easter holidays from school.

# CHAPTER SEVEN

## *The long-serving men on the farm*

A picture in the East Anglian Daily Times gives me the chance to describe the work of each of the men photographed at the Suffolk Show. They had all spent their entire lives working in the village.

Nearest the camera was John Baxter. He was one of two horsemen looking after the horses at Warren Hills, His daily routine was to feed the horses before he had his breakfast, then start work at the same time as the other workers. Both horsemen lived in the other house on the farm at Warren Hills and near the stables. John also looked after the Suffolk Punch Stallion and in the evenings in spring would visit neighbouring farms taking the stallion to serve the mares. This horse always knew when a mare was in season when they were on their travels. John's skills with horses was ploughing, drilling and at haysell and harvest he would be in charge of building the stacks.

During the Second World War men on the farm had been conscripted into the Army, and others joined voluntarily. Women were also joining the forces, with other young women having to do their war work, which included the farm work.

Land Army girls were billeted into the villages and local girls joined in. One such girl was Sybil Symonds. She knew nothing about horses and John had to harness and unharness her horse each day. She also had to lead his horse when he was horse hoeing. Romance blossomed and they married, remaining in the village for the rest of their lives. Next to John is Dick Stringer a tractor driver all his life. I believe he drove a tractor similar to the one in the picture of the 1917 tractor driven by Leonard West.

I remember him driving a caterpillar tractor, which pulled a four-furrow plough, and also other implements, which were twice as big as those pulled by wheel tractors. He also drove the combine harvester when it arrived on the farm in 1947. In the centre is Ernie Fulcher. It would be far too simple to say that he was the gardener and his wife the housekeeper to my grandmother and grandfather at Ivy House, but they were so much more than that. They lived in the centre bungalow in the painting of 1840. Ivy House is to the left.

He started work in Brome Hall Gardens before serving in the First World War. Mrs Fulcher was in charge of the household and she always had a maid to help her. She was the one who reprimanded me if I was in the house with dirty shoes. Meanwhile Grandmother spent much of her time keeping account of farm expenditure and doing all the accounts for the Norfolk farms and the wages for all the stockmen. It was Ernie's job to monitor the work being carried out. He did this using his diplomacy, realising that the stockmen were very much in charge. He was also a Jack of all trades and a master of some, and a leading figure in village affairs.

Sid Brundish, Albert Fulcher, Ernie Fulcher, Dick Stringer and John Baxter, who all completed 50 years work on the farm

Next in line is Albert Fulcher a second cousin of Ernie, who was a cowman at Warren Hills. At the beginning of the Second World War he became a tractor driver. Women were now working with the cows as well as on the farm.

Albert lived in a council house. Nearly all the workers at this time either lived in tied cottages or in council houses; very few owned their own homes.

In Brome and Oakley there had been more than 80 houses sold at the demise of the Estate; 36 of these had passed over to the farm; some had been let, but the majority became tied, which meant that the condition of living in the house was that the tenant had to work on the farm, while the rents were controlled by the Wages Board.

This system was disliked by many of the workers. My observation at the time was that Grandfather was keeping his owned houses in decent repair, but where he was hiring farms, the workers' houses were in a very poor condition, as indeed were some of the houses in the village purchased by the tenants and then because of the Depression they were unable to pay for repairs. Albert had explained this to me after The War and when the Women's Land Army was disbanded, and I asked him to return to the cows.

He explained that bringing up a family before the War was tough. Albert worked with the cows to earn extra money to pay the rent on the council house. He preferred driving a tractor and working in the fields. We paid him the same wage for being a skilled tractor driver, which he continued to be until his retirement.

At the far end of the line is Sid Brundish – another First World War veteran. He had all the old-fashioned skills on the farm: hedge-laying, hand digging land drains, hand hoeing sugar beet, stacking and thatching corn stacks and working the threshing drum.

Sid was the most contented man you could meet. He hardly ever left the village, but perhaps he didn't need to as the village had a shop and a pub at the time. His wife would go to Diss on a Friday on the local bus – the service was well used in those days. Sid spent his spare time in the woods collecting firewood or snaring rabbits.

I asked him one day why he had not gone to Great Yarmouth with the annual Oakley Green Man pub bus outing. His reply was that he had never seen the sea and it did not interest him. I pointed out to him that he must have crossed the English Channel when he was serving in France. He said it was always dark when he crossed and the ship was blacked out, so no, he had not ever seen the sea.

Leslie Aldrich, of Syleham, Suffolk, with his threshing engine and barrel organ, and Jim Elliot, who supervised the threshing on the farm

I include another photo taken about the same time, this time at the village fete. It shows Leslie Aldrich, of Syleham, with his steam engine driving a barrel organ. Leslie did the threshing in the area for many years. The picture also shows Jim Elliot. Jim was a master craftsman and he often had Sid Brundish as his number two.

Sid only had one child in his family but Jim's family consisted of 10. He could turn his hand to almost anything and did piece work whenever possible. He worked much harder than Sid as he needed the money to support his family.

I recall one incident during harvest on Pulham Airfield. I was supervising the building of two corn stacks. Jim with two assistants was building one and Ernie Jolly, with two helpers, was building the other. Jim's stacks were upright and perfect, whilst Ernie's had wooden props all round them and one even collapsed. Grandfather arrived on the scene and I got just as much of the blame as Ernie did. Grandfather told me to get up on the stack and show him how to build it properly.

Although I knew the theory behind building a stack I had never actually built one and it was something of a challenge. I gave Ernie the hardest job which was in the Bullyhole ie pitching the heavy shoves onto the roof. Luckily for me Jim came from his stack to mine three or four times to point out if anything was going wrong. When the stack was finished it remained perfectly upright – the same as his.

This was the only stack I ever built. My solution was to get Putney Calver to build the next one. He had only just started work in the farm and he was scything by hand the borders of the wheat fields to enable the binder to operate. I had seen him stacking on a neighbouring farm and he was quite glad to take the job.

I now had no-one to cut the borders as using a scythe was a skill and from then on the tractor ran down the corn on the edge of the field while cutting the first round.

Poor Ernie never built another corn stack as he was always given the harder work to do. I don't think it did him any harm as he was nearly 100 when I last saw him in a pub in Diss. He looked very fit and accepted another pint which I bought for him.

Alec Lewis's farm 1938, harrowing and drilling with a Smythe drill and his Allis Chalmers combine harvester 1938 the first in the area

# CHAPTER EIGHT

## *My neighbour Alec Lewis*

Arriving in Oakley in the mid 1930s was Alec Lewis. He bought two farms and was an innovative farmer, who pioneered many new ideas in agriculture. He was the first farmer in the area to use a combine harvester in 1938 and he had row crop tractors which were another innovation of the time. The tractors, with adjustable wheels were able to hoe and cultivate between rows of sugar beet and vegetables.

Alec took many pictures in 1938 of farming at this time and these have been passed on to his son David who now runs the farms. The combine cost his father £200 and the tractor £150.

Fordson Tractors at the time were selling for £100. Alec, in post-war Britain, became one of the National Farmers' Union leaders negotiating with the Government in London. He represented Suffolk farmers for many years. His work was instrumental in bringing more prosperous times to farmers as well as creating a secure food supply for the population.

Some years later in 1986 I represented Norfolk farmers in London until 1995 and held various posts. This gave me an insight as to how the wheels of Government worked. Britain was now in the Common Market as it was called then, and we had to keep an eye on the workings of Brussels as well as London. But all was not well in the dairy industry as many farms were leaving.

In 1991 I was the delegate for Norfolk, Suffolk and Cambridgeshire. Numbers of farmers in dairying had reduced in 10 years and I had the same number in all three counties combined as had been in Norfolk alone 10 years previously.

# CHAPTER NINE

## *Grandfather George Flowerdew and his farm in Eye*

My reminiscences of the 20th century would not be complete without mentioning my mother's family who were farming in Eye.

Hannah Arete Flowerdew had two brothers, Ken and Dick, as well as a sister Roa. On his marriage Ken went to Gardner's Farm on the edge of Eye, while Dick farmed in Denham.

I think Grandfather Flowerdew's farm was far more typical of a working farm than that of Surrey West's. Ken was farming with his father. As well as the cropping side of the business there were dairy cows, pigs and chickens. I also remember that bee hives were at both farms too.

He was in charge of the dairy, and each day he would go into Eye with a pony and cart delivering milk, which was in churns with a tap at the base, and the customers would come to the cart with their jugs and he would measure out their requirements. I do not recall milk bottles being used.

The surplus milk would be turned into butter and cheese by Grandmother and women helpers who also collected the eggs from the chickens. Butter, cheese and eggs were also sold from the cart, as well as the farm's honey.

Meanwhile Grandfather was looking after the other enterprises on the farm, although he had a car, he was always driving a motorcycle and sidecar. Each morning he would go to Eye with the sidecar laden with potatoes, fruit and vegetables grown on the farm, and make deliveries to the greengrocer's and various houses.

He enjoyed meeting people and later became Mayor of Eye and was subsequently elected as an Alderman.

Grandfather was one of the founders of the Eye branch of the National Farmers' Union and was Branch Secretary from 1921 until 1945. He had to deal with the Tithe War in the 1930s - an episode in agricultural history, which is now almost forgotten.

Tithe was a tax on farms to pay for the running of the Church of England. Every farmer, whatever his religion had to pay a sum of money to the church commissioners. This was at a time when farming was not profitable and many farmers were unable to pay the tax. The commissioners were getting court orders and bailiffs were seizing livestock and crops off the farms, leaving the farmers bankrupt.

Grandfather, as secretary, was organising farmers' protest meetings to lobby Parliament to repeal the Tithe laws. Roland Rash, of Wortham Manor, was one of the many farmers who decided to make a stand against the tax. He was farming at a loss at the time and did not pay the Tithe. He had a court order against him, and he had stock valued at £702 impounded. His wife was Doreen Wallace, a famous author and she was able to get the publicity in the national press. When the bailiffs – protected by more than 100 policemen – arrived there was a huge band of protesters present.

The protests and the publicity eventually had their effect and an act of Parliament in 1936 reduced the payment of tithe so it could be paid by installments. My father had taken me, as a small boy, to the protest. It must have been quite a peaceful war or he would not have allowed me to be there.

I do recall at this time my Grandfather West protesting to our local parson that his tithe bill was the equivalent of 10 farm workers' wages. Times have changed and now the wage of a country parson is very similar to that of just one farm worker.

Grandfather Flowerdew died in 1947. Kenneth continued, with his wife, to farm at Gardner's Farm until he retired in the 1970s. The last Flowerdew, my cousin Raymond, who was farming at Denham retired very recently.

Today for the first time in 900 years there is not a single member of the Flowerdew family still in agriculture. We are able to trace our ancestors back that far. They moved here from Normandy soon after William The Conqueror. The family at that time had come in possession of a manor in South Norfolk.

The Flowerdews were - at the time of the last Peasants' Revolt led by the brothers Kett in 1549 – farming in the Wymondham area and enclosing land for sheep grazing, thus causing the revolt. About this time my direct ancestor had already had already moved to a farm in Mendlesham, Suffolk, and was therefore not directly involved in the dispute.

A second cousin of mine - now deceased – Ruth Flowerdew – researched her family tree and her findings were that the family farmed in the area all through the 900-year period.

1927 harvest Grandfather George Flowerdew is in the centre.

Dick Flowerdew on motorcycle with milk churn carting whey surplus to butter and cheese making to feed to the pigs.

Ken Flowerdew carrying a sack of sugar beet pulp

Ken Flowerdew with his Oak Lawn Dairy cart

# CHAPTER TEN

## *The farm and the 1939 War*

At the outbreak of World War Two Warren Hills was chosen by the Middlesex Territorial Brigade to be the headquarters of the district searchlight units. It was chosen because it was one of the few farms in the area to have an adequate water and electricity supply.

Searchlights were positioned at regular intervals around the area to enable the RAF to see the enemy aircraft at night. The troops were also preparing for an invasion from the continent. Initially they all lived in tents, but later army huts were erected for storage and living quarters. On Oakley plains to the east the RAF erected a flashing beacon to guide the aircraft to Honington Airbase, near Thetford, at night.

In the autumn of 1940, the leaves came off the trees around the army base and the beacon shone directly on to the huts. A German bomber seeing this target, dropped five bombs. They all missed their target, hitting our chicken huts and landing near the farm. The surviving chickens did not lay any eggs for several days. I believe ours was the only house in the village to be damaged by enemy action. We all heard the bombs whistling down and took shelter under the table.

When I returned to school as an Eye Grammar School pupil after the long summer break just after war broke out in September 1939, I noticed how numbers had doubled. School children were being evacuated from London to rural areas where it was considered safer for them to endure the war. Children from London were in equal number to the local children.

During the winter of 1939 I suffered ill health and spent a time in hospital. When I had recovered enough to leave I then spent time in Southwold, on the coast with my aunt, Aurora Flowerdew who was the district nurse.

I remember many of the local inhabitants had left the area. The town was full of soldiers living in requisitioned halls and hotels where they were being trained.

The roads were full of marching soldiers who were also using the beach and the common as a training ground. I did not return to school until the autumn of 1940. To bring me back to full health I was told to spend as much time outside as possible. This suited me well. Life outside was much better than going to school and at this time there was never a better time to be on the farm as great changes were taking place in agriculture.

War Agricultural Committees were set up with powers to direct farmers to grow crops, which were in the national interest. This meant that land used as pasture had to return to the plough. Crops of wheat, potatoes, vegetables and sugar beet were allocated to each farmer. The dairy cow was the only livestock which was encouraged. Failure to comply with instructions could result in the land coming under the direct control of the committee with the back up of a labour force and machinery. The reason for these powers soon became apparent. German submarines were sinking merchant shipping carrying food supplies. This caused food shortages and rationing had to be imposed on the population.

I think the family anticipated these changes taking place and had purchased extra tractors and machinery, which enabled them to double the arable acreage on the farm.

Being away from school I was able to see these changes at first hand. I used to bike with the shepherds to their sheep on Pulham Airfield. To gain access we had to sign in through the main gate. The area was well protected with armed RAF personnel, anti-aircraft guns were positioned around the base. At the eastern end of the base was an experimental unit testing naval and air force explosives. When these were exploded, the cattle and sheep had to be removed from the area. At the railway junction a goods train would arrive on most days bringing supplies to be dispersed by the miniature railway network. The place was always busy and packed with both RAF and civilian personnel.

The western part of the airfield was not required by the RAF; this area was being cleared of scrub by our workers. The scrub consisted of gorse brambles in long grass and had to be loosened with a steam gyratiller, consisting of a steam engine powering two large rotating drums with tines attached which loosened the roots of the scrub.

Two steam engines fitted with a wire cable and winches hauled a plough or cultivator backwards and forwards across the field. Picture courtesy of the Eastern Daily Press

A barbed-wire entanglement and the concrete bases for a windscreen serving an early non-rigid airship shed can be seen in the foreground of this wartime photograph of the camouflaged Pulham hanger. Missing panels from the wall were blown out by a blast from a bomb which exploded inside the building

The terminus of the standard gauge line inside the air station. The Nissen building replaced an earlier wooden structure

Fragments of crashed aircraft piled at Pulham during the Second World War, the largest dumping ground in the country for crashed aircraft

This was followed by a steam cultivator which brought the resultant bushes to the surface. The debris was then removed enabling ploughing to take place. By early 1941 some 400 acres had been cleared in this way, ploughed and sown with crops.

As well as removing the scrub from the land, the farm workers were cutting the 25 years of growth of the boundary hedges. In these hedges there were numerous small trees. These were converted into fence posts to separate the area, which had been cleared for pasture land. The shepherds were erecting fences to keep livestock within their boundaries. My task with the aid of sheep dogs was to keep the sheep and cattle on the grassland whilst the fences were being erected.

In the summer of 1940 the cattle had to be evacuated from Orford Ness via the beach so that the area could be landmined. The cattle went to Pulham, and as there was not enough grazing left the sheep were transferred to Orford and loaded onto an RAF launch on Orford Quay. They all had to cross the River Alde and had to be lifted on and off the boat by hand.

I did not participate on this operation, but two weeks later we had to evacuate Halvergate Island. I was there that day and I remember it well. To reach Orford we had to pass through the defence lines being prepared for the threatened invasion by Germany. To the east of Wickham Market there were trenches with tank traps and gun emplacements.

The woods were full of troops with tanks and gun carriers. Many civilians were evacuated, our cattle lorries were fitted with a plate to show that we could pass through the area. I still have the plate which was attached to Father's car.

The old farm barge was prepared for the evacuation and the cattle were assembled in the collecting pen on the island. At sea we could see the barrage balloons above a convoy of ships. The first load of cattle were in the middle of the river when there were explosions and gun fire from the direction of the convoy. I guess a German air raid was in progress.

I was on the island at the time and the noise of the explosions caused the cattle on the barge to panic and they rushed up to the landing door, knocking it into the river. The barge sank and the cattle swam out. My father and the other two crew went down with the barge. With the cattle off it, the barge re-emerged with the very wet crew members clinging to the side. George Brinkley, the marshman had a motorboat and brought the three survivors back to the island where we cajoled the rest of the cattle to join the other cattle already in the river. The 70-odd cattle were then guided to the mainland.

This was not the end of our problems as the incoming tide caused the cattle to miss the landing stage and finish up on the mud flats. It took all afternoon to get them back on dry land. I should imagine very few people have witnessed 70 cattle swim a tidal river.

The following day the barge was beached on the mud flats near Orford Quay. The wreck was still there several years later. No livestock ever returned to the island. It is now a breeding ground for avocets and owned by the RSPB.

In 1941 we had to evacuate the sheep from Orford Ness as the Airforce required it for bombing practice. We learnt after the War that Barnes Wallace the inventor of the bouncing bomb used by the Dam Busters, had been transferred from the experimental unit at Pulham to Orford to supervise the development of the bomb.

These sheep were the last left on the farm. With the lack of pasture all the sheep and fat cattle were sold off. The remaining grass on the farms was needed for dairy herds. Pig rearing had also ceased, there were now no imports of animal feeds and the grain grown on the farm was needed for human consumption.

Life back at school in the autumn term seemed much more tame after the summer break. During the air raid warnings all pupils had to go to air raid shelters built in the school grounds. Teaching staff members were short as the younger ones had been called up to join the forces. Some of the playing field had been dug up to grow vegetables for the school canteen and gardening lessons were frequent.

In mid-winter the school's heating system broke down. For nearly a month repairs could not be carried out and we spent our lessons wearing overcoats and gloves. Both the towns of Diss and Eye were bombed; I believe there were casualties, but the bombs did little damage to buildings.

Our evacuees at Warren Hills returned to London where they felt they would be safer in the underground shelters provided in the capital than being in the countryside with no air raid shelters being provided. I remember seeing the results of two air raids on Pulham. The first resulted in bombs hitting the giant hangar, blowing out the sides but only making holes in the roof where the bombs entered.

The second resulted in one of the storage sheds being hit. Luckily on both occasions the sheds were empty. German bombers were frequently seen. On one occasion I witnessed a German Dornier bomber being chased by three Hurricane fighters. It was shot down over Starston.

The War brought great changes to our rural community: the men who were working on farms were being called up into the forces. The Home Guard in Brome and Oakley, had been formed in 1940 and my father was the first commander, but in 1941 a retired Army officer was put in charge.

All went well until the harvest of 1941 when my father decided that harvest had priority over military training. He was dismissed from the service and became a special constable. Most of the men refused to attend parades as harvest was very tiring in those days. The impasse was resolved by the officer in charge resigning and another officer being appointed. Everything from then on went smoothly; the local Home Guard often used to go to the coast to man the defences but never during the harvest season.

In 1941 the area became the centre of a drive to build airfields. Much of the labour force for the construction came from Ireland.

Land on our farm at Snetterton was taken for the building of the first airfield. Land in Fersfield, Tibenham, Thorpe Abbotts and Horham was also being used about this time.

Huge gravel pits, along the Waveney Valley were being excavated to provide the materials for their construction. In three years 16 airfields within a 15-mile radius of Diss and Eye would be constructed, each taking 300 acres of farm land.

In the summer of 1942 my father was informed that our farm in Brome was to become an American Airbase, and American troops would be doing the construction with equipment being imported from The United States of America.

It was during harvest when they arrived. Some American servicemen came from Horham airfield to erect tents. We were still cutting barley with a binder when they arrived. I was operating the binder which was an easy job for a boy and the tractor was driven by Walter Stebbings. As the sheaves of barley were ejected from the binder the Americans moved them to one side to make space for the tents to be erected to accommodate 800 servicemen.

The following day the threshing machine was placed in the field and the barley was threshed. The field was then clear for the servicemen who had previously arrived in Southampton and travelled to Diss railway station. My father had already been informed that the troops were from the southern state of Louisiana, and that they were all black. The officers – who were white – were the technicians and were to be housed in commandeered farm cottages in Eye (these were later demolished to make way for the runway.)

At this time segregation was the norm in the southern states. The local police, including my father, who had already stated there would be no segregation on his farm, had informed the American officers there was no such thing as segregation in England. Jamaicans and English airmen were already working side by side at Pulham. Discussions on this matter took place in the August and the authorities readily agreed with my father. According to the papers recently released this issue was not resolved until the end of September by Washington and London.

The Americans got a warm welcome from a German Aircraft on the night of their arrival. Their Army issue sleeping bags needed padding for comfort and the farm provided them with loads of straw from the recent threshing. No-one told them that black-outs were a necessity at night, and not being used to the cold nights, they set fire to the straw for warmth. The German aircraft flying overhead at the time dropped a canister of incendiary bombs, which exploded over the area. Luckily there were no casualties, but a great deal of panic.

Their training back home in America, had been in dealing with construction equipment and building materials not warfare. The Americans had to wait for their equipment to arrive and in their spare time they soon integrated with the local community. Most of them were from rural communities in the southern states of America and were rural workers, so the working conditions were similar.

After my binder work was finished, I was driving away with the horses and farm wagons and each day had to go to their camp area to get the hay for the horses. The Americans would always load the cart for me. One told me he had never seen a white boy working in the fields at home.

With the Americans in our midst the whole area was extremely active. Fields in the three villages of Brome, Eye and Yaxley became an aerodrome with three runways, hangars and accommodation for 2,500 airmen. The airfield had running water and a sewerage system – something the village was to lack for several years to come.

After harvest it was back to school for me, which involved biking through the area of construction of the airfield every day, dodging bulldozers, jeeps and heavy lorries. It was chaos at first but as the Americans completed their own road network, cycling became less hazardous.

It was early in 1943 when many of the airfields in the area became operational and there was a huge influx of American aircrews and ground staff. Trouble erupted in the evenings when the black troops from Brome intermingled with the servicemen on the other airfields. I suspect this was largely fuelled by the consumption of alcohol.

The local police and military authorities decided to ban the other bases' personnel from the Eye area and the black troops could not go to the Diss area. This only took place in the evenings and every bridge on the rivers Dove and Waveney had American military police stationed there to enforce the order.

The ground crews for the airfield started arriving in late 1943 after the construction company moved to Debach to complete the building of another airfield. The aircraft - four-engined B24 liberators - started arriving early in 1944. Not able to fly the Atlantic direct, they flew via the Caribbean, Brazil and Africa. They had to be refuelled four times. The Diss to Eye road was now closed except for schoolchildren with passes. Other travellers had to go via the Norwich/Ipswich road through Yaxley but this journey was not always possible as some of the aircraft were parked on the other side of the main road, and every time an aircraft crossed the road to reach the runway the road was closed as well.

The Blenheim bomber crash at Warren Hills in March 1940

Plane crash at Brome Swan

American army officers were in charge of the US Engineering Battalion in line outside Church Farm

The army Mess Hall now the Mink Farm, in Brome

B24 bombers ready to take off at the airfield in Eye, early 1944

B17 Fortress bomber at Langton Green, Eye in 1944

The Mustang fighter, which crashed into the Brome village shop in 1944

Here I am aged 15 ready for take off with an American flying crew

The remains of a Hanley Page bomber which blew up after a fire and crashed at Warren Hills in the early 1960s, killing three of the crew of five

There were 10 aircraft crashes in Brome during the War with the loss of 42 lives.

Less than a year into the war, 1940, saw two crashes: The first was a Blenheim Bomber, which had run out of fuel and somersaulted on land in a ploughed field.

The second was a Whitley bomber, which came down in the same field having suffered engine failure. It was laden with bombs at the time, although they did not explode. These were RAF planes and there were no casualties.

In 1943 a Flying Fortress from Thorpe Abbotts crashed on the road killing three local workmen and a horse as well as the crew of 10.

In 1944 two aircraft crashed at the end of the runway, in Brome, after failing to gain height. There were no casualties in the first crash but a fortnight later a plane crashed and exploded killing the crew of 10. A lot of houses had their windows blown out with this explosion.

A few days later a Mustang fighter crashed into the kitchen of the village shop while attempting to land.

The mid-air collision between two bombers with the loss of 17 crew members, 3 parachuted to safety) is still too horrible to think about. The bombs they were carrying on the planes exploded when they hit the ground. One landed on our cattle shed which is no more. In the spring of 1945 another Mustang crashed into a tree behind the farmyard killing the pilot.

I witnessed a Liberator Bomber returning to land with only two engines working. It failed to reach the runway and glided over a row of oak trees knocking the tops out before crashing on the road outside Brome Swan. On my bike I was soon on the scene but by the time I arrived, the plane was ablaze. I was amazed to see all the crew had escaped the inferno, although two of them died shortly afterwards. This crash occurred on the 29th July 1944

It is difficult to explain the enormity of the aerial activity at this period of the War. The RAF were overhead all night and the Americans on the airfield would be warming the engines of their aircraft well before dawn, ready for take-off.

I have the records of the American 8th Airforce, based in East Anglia, at this time and have selected the records for the day of this last crash. It was a typical days operation. Some 1,228 B-17 and B-24 Bombers were dispatched to eight targets. The records say 2,957 tons of bombs were dropped, 17 aircraft did not return and nine crew members were killed – this would include the two members of the Brome Swan crash. Another 26 were injured and 153 crew members went missing. The bombers were escorted by 755 fighters, seven went missing with their pilots.

Who would have thought that I would have had a chance of flying with some of the airmen during the time they were stationed in Brome for the war campaign.

By 1944 there were many changes on the farm, compared with 1939. Grandfather, with the building of Snetterton Airfield on part of the farm, gave up the tenancy of the rest as well as land in East Harling. He also sold two other farms.

The price of land had doubled and he (mistakenly) thought it would go down again after the War was over. Meanwhile the Ministry of Agriculture, as it was called then, had appointed father a livestock distribution officer to the various abattoirs in the area.

Livestock were in very short supply now and there was very little English meat to ration. Tins of Bully Beef and Spam from abroad were included in the ration.

My uncle Dick (mother's brother) lost some of his land on Horham Airfield so he turned to buying poultry, rabbits rooks and moor hens, and sending them to London. These items were not rationed and fetched a high price.

Father was also on police duties as a Special Constable. Both the British and American commanders knew his position and if there was trouble he had direct access to the military police on the base.

With the loss of Orford, Snetterton and the other farms, activities at Pulham and Brome, the farm was well under half the size it was in 1939.

Land Army girls were doing much of the livestock work and Italian prisoners of war were doing much of the manual work on the farm. There was a prisoner of war camp at Redgrave Park, Suffolk, with many inmates. At first they had armed guards, but this was soon found to be unnecessary and they used to come onto the farm in a covered lorry driven by a civilian. The first thing the gang would do in winter was to search for firewood and light a fire to keep warm. Work was not their strong point – providing cigarettes and milk did help. I remember going back with my father to the camp with a prisoner who was the ringleader of a go-slow movement.

Father reported his antics and he was placed in a cell on reduced rations. The following day the work rate was greatly increased.

When Italy came out of the War, they were no longer prisoners of war and many of them were able to return home. Many of those who were unable to return home because the Germans still occupied northern Italy, continued to work on the farms, some went into lodgings whilst others were given accommodation in disused Army huts. The PoW camp now housed German prisoners of war.

At the age of 16 we had to register for the services and encouraged to join Army or Navy cadets. I had already joined the Air Training Corps, and had been issued with a uniform, sometimes we were allowed to fly. My first flight was from Shepherd's Grove, near Stanton.

I was put aboard a Sterling bomber,which was engaged in taking off towing an army glider containing about 26 troops with their equipment.

Three days later the sky was full of these planes towing gliders. They were bound for the Arnhem Landing. Living in the vicinity of the airfield and wearing my uniform, I was able to persuade the American pilots to take me on their engine testing flights.

There was a link trainer in the maintenance shed, which had all the controls in the cockpit and a flight simulator.

Sitting in this trainer I learned all the controls, and once in the air the pilots sometimes allowed me to fly the plane. I had to keep the plane at a constant 10,000 feet

On one occasion I was alone at the controls in the cockpit as the pilot and co-pilot went to the rear of the plane to play cards. The other airmen playing cards panicked when they saw their pilot and co-pilot sitting down with them. One airman looked forward to the cockpit but could see no-one at the controls. I was very small at the time, being only 15-years-old, and I was hidden from view by the seat.

Seeing the countryside from the air was a new experience for me. Airfields in Norfolk and Suffolk were thick on the ground. Our farm at Pulham could be seen miles away with its huge bomb-battered hangar.

Next to the hangar was a huge scrap yard of crashed aircraft, which were piled three high and spread over 25 acres. Planes from all over East Anglia were brought here. Some were British, some German, but most were American. This aircraft graveyard was at the time believed to be the largest in the country.

One flight I was on, the pilot and crew were not satisfied with the planes' performance, so on landing he took it to the area on the airfield where aircraft were dismantled. This was on a Saturday, and on the following Monday on going to school I noticed the plane being broken up ready for Pulham, at the time there were more aircraft than flying crews available.

# CHAPTER ELEVEN

## *Starting work on the farm*

The Americans left the airbase in July 1945, almost immediately civilian contractors who had previously been building airfields moved in with orders to demolish all empty buildings which were mostly Nissen huts. Housing was in very short supply at the time and quite a number of families decided to squat in the best huts. On the farm, realising what was happening we occupied some storage sheds. I joined in by going to Apthorpe's sale in Diss and buying some breeding pigs – which appreciated their new living quarters. I had selected the officers' huts for them as accommodation.

My problem was that pig food was rationed and only obtainable by established pig rearers and this did not include myself. Grandfather said I could use the mill at nights – the Ministry would not miss the grain. To supplement this grain I was able to buy two lorry loads of tinned food, which had been condemned by the Ministry because the tins were rusty. The contents were wholesome and readily appreciated by the pigs. The only snag being there were 50,000 tins to open. A rapid tin opening mechanism was devised with two German PoWs having the task.

In 1946 a ship load of Iraq barley (unrationed) arrived in Yarmouth at a cost of £17-00 a ton. That soon solved the pig food ration problem.

In 1945 I had left school and started work on the farm. Whilst at school and biking three miles to Eye every day I picked up quite a bit of knowledge about how a farm operated.

I had many varied tasks to begin with, even in the spring of 1945, I was given the task of overseeing the German PoWs hoeing sugar beet, by providing them with hoes each morning. They were very willing workers, some could speak English, but very few knew how to hoe sugar beet, so I had to show them what to do.

Germany was in ruins and many PoWs did not know what had happened to their families, especially those who had been living in what was now the Russian zone. They knew that with good behaviour and hard work their repatriation would be speeded up.

I recall one amusing incident: The Germans were eating their meal in a field next to the American refuse dump. The dump was being unloaded and flattened by American Army troops who had committed breaches of discipline. They were supervised by American Military Police equipped with long batons. The troops were being forced to work at the double – an early version of Guantanimo Bay. The Germans, rather bemused by all this, wryly asked me: "Who had won the war Germany or America?'

At harvest time we had a gang of the Hitler Youth on the farm. They were very young, about the same age as I was. To start with they were arrogant, saying they were the master race. In fact they did not believe Germany had lost the war, thinking it was just British propaganda.

I was amazed that they had been released from the camp. Their attitude was not tolerated by the farm staff, most of whom had been in the Home Guard, or were returning ex-servicemen.

The strong pressure of our workforce, who were still appaled by the disclosure of the concentration camps, soon brought them to heel. Being very young their minds had become twisted by 12 years of Nazi indoctrination. I hope their 14 days bringing in our harvest made them more normal citizens when they returned home.

In 1946 I took over the duties of being wages clerk for the workers on the farm with the exception of the stockmen. There were 46 on the list, all of them men as the women's Land Army had been disbanded and there was no longer PoW labour. The sugar beet crop was still labour intensive and the grain crops still had to be hand hoed. It would be a few more years before the use of sprays came to eliminate weeds from the sugar beet and grain.

Many of the returning servicemen were looking for work, but some had memories of the hard hand work of pre-war days and decided to look for employment away from the farm.

Ted Hardy was the village blacksmith in Scole before he was called into the Army. My father had brought the Anvil bellows and the rest of the equipment to Warren Hill. Ted was offered his old job back but he declined. He had been a lorry driver during the War and became one of the farm lorry drivers instead.

Civilian employees on the airbases were now out of work and some of them were on my list of employees. Brome Airfield was now deserted and was being brought back into cultivation between the runways. To reduce the labour force in the dairy herds we were building milking parlours. I was involved in the change over on the first farm Warren Hills in 1946

Once they were in operation the cows were fed together in yards. They no longer had to be tethered individually, the milk was piped directly to the dairies. There was no longer the need to carry heavy milk buckets. A snag to this system was the horns on the cows. Now they were being fed together they used their horns to bully each other so they had to have their horns removed – a very bloody task indeed.

The heifers coming into the herd had already been dehorned at a few days old. Once the change over was complete at Warren Hills we then made the necessary changes on each farm until milk production was fully mechanised on all the farms.

Having witnessed the first change over I was put in charge of subsequent changes. We still had a labour force at Pulham, but tractors and machinery were still being interchanged between the Suffolk farms and then onto Pulham, in Norfolk.

Suffolk being light land usually had work nearly completed before the heavy clay land of Pulham could be cultivated. This also applied to the harvest. Barley was a light land crop and the following heavy land was good wheat growing land.

I would go to Pulham most days taking supplies in the Army truck, and supervising the Pulham workforce. Whilst there I would inspect the young cattle on the pastures.

Before the War Grandfather always went to North Devon each autumn to purchase young Devon beef cattle for fattening, in a week he would buy enough to fill a train. In 1946 he went with my father who drove him round the farms, they were well-known and in three days they had filled a train. Ernie Fulcher, with some help, had the task of unloading them and getting them along the road to the Hoxne marshes. Three days later my father rang to inform me that another load was on the way.

The next morning I told Ernie that another load was coming in that day. He was furious, saying he had no grazing left. We agreed that they would have to go to Pulham Airfield. The only spare pasture was near Rushall village, here there was a locked Air Ministry Gate.

I went to the main gate, a further mile up the road to get the key. The inspector of the security guards refused to hand it over to me, saying it could only be opened in an emergency.

I had no intention of going through that main gate and getting new cattle mixing with cattle already on the station, So the cattle were walked through Scole and Dickleburgh to Rushall where we moved the fencing around the locked gate by uprooting it with a chain and the Army truck.

We were replacing the fence once the cattle were through on the meadow when the inspector and two wardens arrived. He was furious. He informed me that he was formerly a Regiment Sergeant Major and I should be in the Army and get more discipline instilled into me and he was reporting me to the station commander.

I told him that our farm had been driving cattle through the gate for 30 years. If we could use it through two world wars, why was security more important in peace time than during hostilities. I did not hear anything further on the incident.

Meanwhile in Suffolk, my father could see that changes would take place on the arable side of our business. We were expecting a 12-foot combine harvester and a large crawler tractor. Fields would have to be enlarged.

Bulldozers and drainage machines came onto the farm, hired in from contractors. Work started in 1946 and continued for a further 10 years. They removed the hedges and banks of the small arable fields. At the beginning of the operation there were 116 small arable fields each averaging 8½ acres. After 10 years there were 32 fields averaging 31 acres.

At the same time we were engaged in bringing the airfield sites on Brome Airfield back into cultivation. Storage and Nissen Hut bases were broken up and removed as well as some roadways. The debris was used to construct new roadways and concrete hard standings. Some 50 acres of derelict land was recovered

I have examined the tithe maps of 1838 and little had changed in field size for 100 years. The hedges being removed were very scruffy and riddled with rabbits. The only trees were dead elms.

The oaks and ash trees had all been felled in 1920 before the sale of the estate.

My mother was very saddened when these trees disappeared and every winter she would make sure we planted oaks and ash saplings in field corners. These trees are now 60 years old and are a feature of the village landscape.

Being livestock farmers we have also retained and managed the boundary hedgerows, which are a good habitat for the birds.

# CHAPTER TWELVE

## *The year 1947 and beyond*

I would imagine any person of my age who had an outdoor occupation would never forget the weather of 1947. It was the worst year of the century. In my diary for that year I was apparently staying in London with relatives. The London buses were not running in the first week of January because they were frozen in their garages – apparently there was a shortage of anti-freeze.

On returning home we had a 20-acre field of sugar beet still to lift and harvest. The beet were frozen in the ground and they would remain there until the end of March. There was skating on Diss Mere and Dickleburgh Moor all that month and in the last week there were snowstorms which blocked all the roads. Snow ploughs were very crude in those days and they could not cope with the high snowdrifts.

Feeding the cattle was a nightmare. They had to be let out of the yards to drink from the ponds because their drinking troughs were frozen solid. We had some cattle outside on meadows in Hoxne and they would shelter under hedges and live on hay straw and frozen sugar beet tops. They drank water from the river. The ice had to be smashed with a sledgehammer each morning. That month I walked across the River Waveney to Thorpe Abbotts. March was the worst month of all: there was a snowstorm and blizzard in the first week which lasted for 48 hours. It has been recorded that nearly 25% of the sheep in Britain died in that storm. Snowdrifts in Wales were 24 feet high with sheep being buried in them.

There was a sudden thaw in the third week of March. The ground, having been frozen solid, now thawed and water gushed off the land. At Warren Hills we had water pouring into the back door and out thought the front door. The River Waveney rose to the highest levels I have ever seen it. The worst flooding of all was in the Fens. The river banks all burst and thousands of acres went under five feet of water. Our troubles were not over because on the last day of the month there was a gale, which blew the roofs off two cattle yards and a barn, sending them into the next-door field. Luckily no cattle were injured, but the roofs went missing.

Drilling conditions were very difficult that year. Where the snow had drifted it became too wet to drill. These conditions affected the whole country. The national wheat yield for the year was .78 of a ton – about 50% of the previous year.

There was still more trouble to come: in late July I was in the middle of a field in Warren Hills when it became very dark. A thunderstorm was on the way. I looked round and saw what appeared to be a solid wall of ice approaching. I ran as hard as I could back to the farm. We had a hail storm, but it was nothing compared to the storm that hit Thrandeston and Palgrave, in Suffolk, where there were hailstones as large as golf balls.

Charles Augustus surveying his crop of sprouts

On Grandfather West's death his coffin was conveyed from Ivy House Farm to Oakley Church by a 90 year old horse drawn wagon originally owned by Great Grandfather James in Sussex

The last year of using the harvest binder 1960, on the binder is my late brother Adrian holding a very young nephew Duncan

C A West and Son staff dinner, 1955, on the occasion of my brother Michael's wedding to Jean Beales. In a very austere Diss Corn Hall, Charlie Gardiner of the Coffee Tavern opposite was the caterer

First attempt at mechanical sugar beet harvesting. Hudson 6 row topper followed by a side rake and finishing with 3 two row cleaner lifters. 5 tractors and drivers replacing 20 manual workers. The end of manually harvesting sugar beet

Combine Harvesters on the farm 1950s

Crops were devastated, chickens were killed and Strudwick's Glasshouses in Palgrave had nearly all the panes smashed. This was the first year we operated a combine harvester but there was nothing to harvest in the area around Brome Swan.

In 1947 an act of parliament was passed called the Agriculture Support Act. This was destined to transform British farming. Food had been rationed in Britain for eight years and was to last for another five years. The act enabled farmers to get grants and subsidies to help them modernise and increase food production.

There was a shortage of food worldwide. In the next 10 years I was to witness first hand a fundamental change in British agriculture and the rural economy greater than changes that had occurred in the previous 200 years. Factories in the towns were converting from producing war weapons to agricultural machinery. In Scotland a factory in Kilmarnock was mass producing Massey Harris Combines.

David Brown Tractors, Ferguson Tractors and Ford Tractors in Yorkshire, Coventry and Dagenham were all running at full tilt. All these tractors were undergoing fundamental design changes. The tractor was no longer a machine hauling horsedrawn farm implements. Hydraulics and power drives meant that farm machinery was being designed to become an integral part of the tractor

At Ipswich, the Ransome's factory was rapidly expanding, mass producing ploughs and farm machinery. Their manufacture of threshing machines was converted to building combine harvesters. The Fison fertiliser factory, also in Ipswich, was greatly expanded to cope with the demand for artificial fertilisers. This company was also a pioneer in the manufacture of weed killers and pesticides.

In Debenham the Bloomfield family quickly foreseeing the developments, changed their business from threshing machines and steam engines to combine harvesters and tractor implements.

They converted our airfield buildings on Brome Airfield to a grain store and installed equipment which could cope with the handling and drying of grain. We also moved the feed mill from Warren Hills to a site on the airfield.

Some of the grain was being fed to the livestock after being mixed with other ingredients. In the next 10 years we increased to operating four combines. Threshing was now confined to the history books.

In Diss, garage agents W D Chitty soon realised that the agricultural machinery business was rapidly expanding. William Chitty's son Ron was the driving force. The firm was the main agent for Ford Tractors a leading manufacturer worldwide. Ron built two large factories: Diss Engineers and Diss Foundry on what was Grandfather's former site in Diss – now Morrisons' supermarket.

The coming of the Ferguson tractor at this time was to revolutionise British farming. This was a small tractor designed to take a two-furrow plough and all the various implements including a fore end loader. The Ferguson system enabled farmers with a limited acreage to continue to farm economically.

The tractor did not tire and it was not long before it replaced the horse. And with the loader, the hard lifting by manual labour was eliminated. We continued with Ford tractors as they were more powerful and useful on a large farm. Sugar beet was very labour intensive to sow, hoe and harvest.

A company in Stanton was developing a single row sugar beet harvester at Stanton called the Catchpole Sugarbeet Harvester. This did not suit our method of harvesting, we, like many other livestock farmers, needed the crowns for cattle feeding. Ford brought out a two-row sugar beet lifter incorporating a spinning cleaning mechanism. At first it was not too successful and I could see some modifications were needed.

Ron Chitty and Diss engineers soon got the spinner working successfully, but the only snag now was the necessity to still top the beet. The following year we had precision drills and tractor hoes, making hand hoeing and the singling of the beet much easier.

Ford introduced The Hudson six-row sugar beet topper followed by a side rake then three Ford spinners. This finished the drudgery for farm workers in some respects, but the beet still needed to be loaded into trailers with forks.

With other employment now available away from agriculture, workers were no longer prepared to work under the harsh conditions of manual hoeing and harvesting. Those remaining mostly became tractor drivers and were operating sophisticated farm machinery.

At the end of the War I left the Air Training Corps as I no longer had the desire to be a pilot in the RAF. Farming was now my ambition. All the other people with similar ideas were joining the Young Farmers' Club. I joined the Diss branch. Farm visits and talks on agriculture were all in their annual programme.

There was a social side as well and the club had a reputation for being a matrimonial agency as well. So it was fitting that I should meet my future wife at Diss Young Farmers' Club.

Sylvia Noble was working in the office of Blooms Nursery, in Bressingham. Alan Bloom the owner, had been working in Canada and on his return to England Sylvia became his secretary. Even back then you could see what a successful business Alan was going to create from small beginnings.

Sylvia and I married in April, 1952 and moved into the farmhouse at Church Farm, in Brome. Having been in charge of the office at the nursery, she was very experienced to take over the office work on the farm.

The following year the remains of Brome Hall Estate came on the market. Grandfather went to the sale to purchase the land and farm on which he was a tenant. There were very few bids for the hall itself and the extensive grounds. The hall stood in 16 acres of gardens and the surrounding park and woods covered 53 acres. Brome Avenue, a tree-lined private one-mile road linking Brome and Eye covered a further six acres. He bought all the land as well as the hall, park and avenue. He did not bid for the Lordship of the Manor, which was sold for £75, stating it was only a piece of paper.

At first we thought the hall and its grounds, and park covering 70 acres was a bit of a white elephant. Most of the timber of any value had been felled by previous owners and had not been replanted. The hall itself had become semi-derelict. The whole area had been used by the Army during the War.

After surveying the stables and other out buildings beside the hall, we decided they were in better condition than the buildings on Home Farm, next door, where we were still milking in semi-derelict buildings, as tenants.

A milking parlour was installed in the stables and other buildings were converted to storage and livestock cover at very little cost. The cows were moved from the old farm buildings and supplemented with the dairy herd from Pulham where the cow shed was also in desperate need of repair. This was our last modernising of the dairy units until 1970 when it was decided to amalgamate

the milking parlours into one herringbone unit with modern equipment. This reduced our labour requirements for milking by 70% and we still produced the same amount of milk.

Four years after I started on the farm, in 1945, my brother Michael joined us and three years after the sale of Brome Hall Farm, in 1956, neighbouring Abbey Farm on the edge of Eye came on the market. With the younger generation wanting to expand, this was purchased, and shortly after that Michael married and moved into the farmhouse.

My wife pictured in the middle at Blooms Nurseries, May 1950

# CHAPTER THIRTEEN
## *Death of a grandfather*

Grandfather West died in 1958 at the age of 89. Shortly before his death he was being chauffeured around the farm most days. As well as my father at this time my two younger brothers and my cousin, Roger Prior, were on the farm. Grandfather West had a vision of the family carrying on where he left off.

Being the eldest of the grandsons I felt I should branch out and expand the business. Shortly after his death Fernleigh Farm, Tivetshall was purchased in the vicinity of the 850-acre tenanted farm at Pulham. I was making preparations to move into the purchased farmhouse at Tivetshall with Sylvia when tragedy struck and my brother, Michael was killed in an accident, leaving a widow, Jean, and his two-year-old son Duncan. We delayed the move until family life returned to normal, but two years after Michael's death, tragedy struck again, this time taking my younger brother Adrian, who was killed in a car crash at the Pulham Crossroads.

The loss of his father and the death of two of his three sons left my father – and of course, my mother – devastated. The future dreams of the family business seemed to be blown off course. There was also the payment of death duties, which were a serious issue at the time. Sylvia and I remained at Brome, where we still live.

Jean eventually married Peter Dale and moved to the Tivetshall farmhouse with her young son.

At the same time Pulham Airfield was closing down. Buildings and railway tracks were all auctioned as the site had to be cleared in time for the sale of the land and the remaining property. In 1962 I bought the tenanted land, which included eight houses, which were all in rather a sad state of repair. It had been a difficult decision to decide to buy the farm. Father, with his tax commitments, was opposed. I managed to persuade the bank that, as a tenant, I had an advantage over other prospective buyers.

At the time of the purchase, only half the land had been cleared for cultivation. Clearing the other half turned out to be a greater challenge than that experienced on Brome Airfield, where the clearance of concrete bases of Nissen hut sites was the main task.

At Pulham the underground drainage system of 1914 construction was in urgent need of repair. The securing bases for the airships, some 50 of them, were between six and nine cubic feet of concrete with huge steel attachments weighing more than 20 tons. We managed to bury them in holes with five feet of soil on top of them. The concrete bases of the munition sheds and the material from the two miles of railway track were used to build roadways. Once cleared the whole farm became arable land.

We were now in a position to store grain in the airfields maintenance sheds. The bomb-proof walls were ideal for grain storage after it had been dried by purchasing a new continuous flow-grain drier – a big improvement on our Brome grain drying system.

Small woods and hedges were planted. I recall the bleakness of the area in the 1930s. I believe this planting in the last 50 years has created a pleasant landscape – despite the existence of the ruins of the old airbase.

Meanwhile back in Suffolk, my cousin Roger Prior and his parents, living in Ivy House, had become farmers on the Brome Hall Farm. My parents had inherited Brome Hall. It was in a very bad state of repair as very little maintenance work had been carried out on it in the last 50 years. A restoration grant was applied for and we were confident that it would be forthcoming. We were wrong.

Many public bodies were approached, but finally no public money was forthcoming. The reason given was that Sir Edward Kerrison had turned the hall into a Victorian building and at that time there was no grant money available for buildings of that period. Permission was granted for the hall to be demolished and my parents built a modern house on the site and also restored the gardens.

In the 1960s we were employing a large labour force. With the improvements in agricultural machinery; increasing use of fungicides, herbicides and insecticides and also plant breeding, out put in agriculture was increasing every year. The same improvements were occurring in livestock production. The days of mixed production on farms which had been prevalent and sustainable for the last half century were being replaced with specialised poultry, pig and cattle production units.

We were down to three dairy units and we were also retaining the male calves for beef fattening. Male cattle from the dairy units would not fatten well on grass, but would grow very quickly when fed mainly on a grain diet. The development of antibiotics, feed rations and breeding improvements led to each dairy cow producing more milk. The frozen food industry was rapidly expanding as well and a group of farmers in our area agreed to form a co-operative to grow and process green peas. Harvesting machinery was bought and static pea viners were installed on the airfield at Brome.

Here the peas were shelled and cooled with ice and transported to the Birds Eye freezing factory in Lowestoft. The pea vine minus the peas made good silage for cattle feed. Not every farmer had cattle and the vines being on our farm, meant that we collected the surplus and clamped it. This was a good feed and meant that we no longer needed the crowns of the sugar beet.

At this time I was keen to keep up with innovations which were taking place in food production. Research was taking place throughout western Europe where farming conditions were similar to ours. Farmers' groups were organising tours to visit our European neighbours. I endeavoured to join a group on most years. I was also appointed onto the Norfolk Agricultural Executive Committee and represented the Central Southern Area. Our task was to liaise between the farming community and the various Government agricultural departments and research bodies.

In 1965 our farm was selected for the National Sugar Beet Demonstration. This entailed the British Sugar Corporation taking a 200-acre block of land: 40 acres for car parking and the remainder for experiments, seeding, cultivating and harvesting sugar beet. This was quite an experience for me. Meeting the leading botanists, scientists and manufacturers in the industry. My impression was that about half the participants were from Europe and the United States. All the work was carried out by the Corporation. I became a member of the planning committee, meeting all the boffins was a chance to gain more knowledge.

Cutting and harvesting green peas ready for delivery to the Birds Eye factory in Lowestoft

Duke, the last Suffolk Punch on the farm, he was previously in Charlie Saunders' prize winning six horse wagon team at many Agricultural Shows

The last stubble burning on the farm

Cows going for milking for the last time at Church Farm in 1996

My son Andrew loading the last lot of pigs onto a trailer for market

The demonstrations were open to the farm growers for two days in the spring and another two days in the autumn. The turn out was more than 1,000 on each day. At this time Mono Germ seed was available and drilled by precision drills and selective weed sprays were used. The hard work of hand hoeing the crop was eliminated.

Most experiments were successful, but there were one or two disasters. Sprays were available as was advice on drilling techniques. In the Autumn all the harvesters were tested against each other and for the first time there was a self-propelled harvester and a number of six-row multi-stage harvesters. By now most of the drudgery of the sugar beet crop had been drastically reduced.

In 1978 the demonstration returned to the farm. In the intervening years there had been a big advance in technology and subsequently an increase in yields. Once again I found it very stimulating to take part.

Once more many farmers turned up on the four open days. We bought a multi-row self-propelled sugar beet harvester that year as well as a 15-row precision drill. With the improvement of weed sprays as well the crop was now fully mechanised – it took 30 years of experimentation to reach that point.

Great changes were also taking place in vegetable production. Birds Eye closed the pea vining plant on the airfield, preferring to process their peas at a factory in Lowestoft. They demanded the crop reach their coastal destination within 90 minutes of vining. Our group did its maths and discovered lorries would have to leave the fields every 20 minutes.

To harvest a load of shelled peas meant the purchase by the group of five giant pea viners which would need to be towed around the pea fields by large four-wheel drive tractors. We joined forces with the Mendlesham Group. There were 25 farmers in our group, their farms stretching from Mendlesham in Suffolk to Tibenham in Norfolk.

I was given the task of organising road transport and hired 28 lorries with 56 drivers. We were working the viners 21 hours a day. The system worked surprisingly well, but caused considerable hold-ups on the road network in the area. When we moved from one farm to the next there was a convoy of 12 tractors towing cutting and harvesting equipment and mobile workshops and trailers.

Other crops grown by the group included dwarf beans and Brussell sprouts all for the freezing industry.

The changes in the pea harvesting industry meant that we no longer had access to the pea haulm – or waste. I had noticed the harvesting of whole crop maize for animal feed in central France had moved into Holland and Germany. These two countries had developed varieties, which would thrive in colder climates, similar to ours. The continental countries had also developed efficient machinery for harvesting the crop. We took the plunge and growing maize for the winter livestock feed proved very successful. My father died in 1981, at the time as well as myself there were three of his grandsons on the farm. My eldest son Graham was married and farming the Abbey Farm, at Eye. My eldest daughter Celia was teaching on a large cattle ranch in Australia. My son Andrew was still at home at Church Farm, along with my youngest daughter Karen. Meanwhile my nephew Duncan was living at Warren Hills.

Twenty-nine years on things have changed again and continue to change. Except for the marshes on the Rivers Dove and Waveney where cattle are still grazed, all the farm land is now arable with a wide range of crops: wheat, barley, sugar beet, peas, rape and herbs. The pigs and dairy cows have all gone.

Present day scenes, Waveney Valley winter time, Peter West feeding Long Horn Pedigree Bulls

Waverney Valley, summer scene. Thorpe Abbots in the distance.

Andrew West checking parsley re-growth – sewn in April it is ready in July

Duncan West (left) with operator Colin Pearce

Crop yields have greatly increased and the performance of tractors and farm machinery has much improved. On the farm there are eight full-time employees, who are all highly skilled in operating the sophisticated machinery. The days of the clod-hopping farm worker are long gone.

There is also a full time farm secretary, who has to cope with masses of Government forms and bureaucracy and during the summer harvest of the herbs more labour is required and this side of the business is led by my son Andrew, who lives at Warren Hills with his wife Jo and their two children George and Jessica - the fifth generation to do so.

Duncan and his wife Claire live on the south Norfolk farm in Pulham. Sylvia and I help out when we are needed. My daughter Celia and her husband Darren have cattle stations in Queensland and New South Wales. They have two grown up children Luke and Clare. Karen, her husband Mark and their two children Rebecca and Henry, are journalists and live in Tivetshall.

# EPILOGUE

It is difficult for me to predict the future of agriculture. Unless there is more co-operation between the Agriculture and Environment departments, I believe the needs of the public will not be met. We live in a world where common sense as well as scientific knowledge is needed.

I have tried to record a picture of the local area where my ancestors and I have lived, alongside the many changes that have taken place over several decades.

Diss is still described as a market town, but it is no longer the centre of the farming industry in this area. It has many new houses, supermarkets and commercial industries, which are unrelated to the area. The charm that Sir John Betjeman found is still there, but hidden by the vast increase of road traffic.

Meanwhile despite many changes, the towns of Eye, Harleston and the surrounding villages, have retained their rural character.

There has been an influx of newcomers and many have left the area. While it is always a shame to see people move away, the people who have taken their place and bought their houses, have settled in and mixed well with the rest of us – resulting in a very pleasant place to live work and see out my retirement.

# ACKNOWLEDGMENTS

Much of what I have compiled in this book has come from my parents' family documents and photographs, namely the Wests and the Flowerdews, which have accumulated over many years. I have also drawn on memories from villagers and townsfolk in the Norfolk and Suffolk border area, whom I have encountered during my lifetime.

I must make special mention of my daughter Karen Hindle and local historian and author Stephen Govier, who with their literary experience, have assisted me in compiling my notes into some sort of order.

My thanks also go to David Lewis, who provided the farm photographs taken by his father in 1938; Eric King, who provided details of Brome Hall and Oakley Park; The Clear Alger Foundation for the historic photo of Church Farm, our home for nearly 60 years.

Thanks also for photographs and articles taken from the East Anglian Daily Times and Eastern Daily Press and from the book Pulham Pigs by Gordon Kinsey; Fernhurst (Sussex) Historical Society, and Eric Swain, English contact for the 490th Bomb Group 8th Air Force USAAF. Dennis Cross for loan of post card.

I leave my last thank you to my wife Sylvia, who has been my support and companion for nearly 60 years.